POLLOKSHIELDS

—Historical Guide and Heritage Walk—

Pollokshields Burgh Hall (Cordelia Oliver).

Ronald Smith

First published in the United Kingdom
in 1998 by Glasgow City Council,
City Chambers, Glasgow, G2 1DU.
ISBN 0 906169 52 6
© 1998 – Glasgow City Council.
Printed by Cordfall Ltd, Glasgow.

Foreword

Pollokshields is an attractive nineteenth century suburban area with 15,000 residents, only about three kilometres or two miles south-west of Glasgow's City Centre.

It is easily reached by public transport – there is a frequent and convenient train service between Glasgow Central and Maxwell Park Stations, the latter being the starting and finishing point of the Heritage Walk. At intermediate points on the route, access can also be gained to Dumbreck Station on the Paisley Canal Line and to Pollokshields East and Pollokshields West Stations on the Cathcart Circle for a quick return journey.

This guide is the second in a new series of local historical guides and heritage walks being produced for interesting parts of Glasgow's south side. The first – relating to Queen's Park and the surrounding area – was published early in 1997. It is hoped that the Gorbals and other selected areas will have similar coverage by 1999 when the city celebrates its status as UK City of Architecture and Design.

General information on the city and the Clyde Valley can be obtained from the city's Tourist Information Centre, now situated on the south side of George Square, while more detailed local knowledge can be gained from the list of references at the end of this guide.

The route of the Heritage Walk is shown on the map on the centre pages. The main part of the walk is focussed on the more intensively developed south and east parts of Pollokshields, with an option to continue with the exploration of the more leafy areas, either as an extension to the walk or by car or bicycle. Some of the properties are set back from the public footpath; in these instances, care should be taken to respect the privacy of owners and occupiers.

Cover photograph:- Maxwell Park and Pollokshields Burgh Hall from the air (Pollokshields Heritage).

"**POLLOCKSHIELDS,** a fashionable, suburban, post-office village, in the parish of Govan. It stands about three-quarters of a mile west of Port Eglinton in Gorbals. It extends along a country road, amid rural environs, a few yards south of the Glasgow and Johnstone Canal and Glasgow and Paisley Railway, and nearly parallel to them. It is of quite recent erection, and consists almost wholly of villas and ornate cottages, along both sides of the road. Each ... has its own enclosure, with parterres or bits of lawn; nearly all are elegant or pretentious in their architecture, displaying prominent features, sometimes elaborate ones, of the most admired orders of architecture; and yet scarcely any two are alike in style, while some are so ambitious as to display a blending of styles. The place is sometimes called the Shields."

The above extract, from *The Imperial Gazetteer of Scotland*, (c. 1867), gives a flavour of Pollokshields in its early days. The spelling, 'Pollockshields', is as originally printed. More contemporary with the Ordnance Survey map on page 9 is the description of the developing village of Pollokshields given in Hugh MacDonald's *Rambles Round Glasgow* (1854):

"The picturesque little village of Pollokshields has recently sprung into existence, with a degree of rapidity which fairly rivals the go-a-head Yankee system of town development. This miniature community is composed of elegant cottages and villas, each edifice having its own belt of garden-ground walled in, and tastefully planted in front with flowers and shrubs, and in the rear with kitchen vegetables. The greatest variety of architectural taste, moreover, seems to prevail in this rising suburban settlement. Some two score or so of (houses) are already erected, or are in process of erection, and scarcely two of them are similar in design or construction. Each individual proprietor seems to have had his own ideal in 'stone and lime' and every man's house is as unlike his neighbour's as possible. Should the same determined diversity of style continue to prevail, *Loudon's Encyclopedia of Cottage Architecture* must soon become a dead letter, so far as Glasgow is concerned, as a walk through Pollokshields will be as instructive to the student as a perusal of that ponderous though valuable volume, with its endless disquisitions on projecting porches, ornamental chimney-stalks, peaked gables, rustic arcades, and mullioned windows. It must be admitted, however, that so far as it has gone this variety has, on the whole, an exceedingly pleasing and picturesque effect, and that we know few places in the vicinity of our City where we would more readily wish for a snug cottage home, if 'the lamp of Alladin' were for a brief period ours".

Contents

*The Pond,
Maxwell Park.*

POLLOKSHIELDS

Introduction

Pollokshields has evolved over the last 150 years as a relatively affluent suburb of the city of Glasgow. Its development was promoted by the original landowners, the Maxwells of Nether Pollok, who had been resident in Pollok House since the 18th century. Their association with the area goes back to 1270 and their earliest extant residence, Haggs Castle (No. 26 in this guide), dates from 1585. From the 18th century, the Maxwells resided at Pollok House where the family still retains an apartment, in what is now Pollok Country Park.

The Beginnings of Pollokshields

Pollokshields was the brainchild of the last Sir John Maxwell, the 8th baronet, and his successors, Sir William Stirling Maxwell and Sir John Stirling Maxwell. In 1849, Sir John Maxwell commissioned the Edinburgh-based architect, David Rhind (designer of the Scott Monument in the centre of George Square, Glasgow), to draw up new plans for development on the open fields to the south of the Glasgow, Paisley & Ardrossan Canal (later replaced by the Paisley Canal railway line).

From this beginning, the parts of Pollokshields east and west of Shields Road were to assume different characteristics. Although Rhind proposed some formality in the layout of part of the western sector (as shown on the plan on the following page), the rest was given over to free-standing villas and winding boulevards, breaking with the traditional Glasgow grid-iron pattern of streets. East of Shields Road, the proposed layout was more formal, consisting of streets of terraced housing centred on communal gardens.

In practice, very little of Rhind's suggested layout was implemented. But, if anything, the density distinction between west and east was reinforced in what was actually built. The western area was exclusively developed for villas, effectively a planned garden suburb which considerably predated the 'Garden City' movement and the celebrated examples of Letchworth (1903) and Welwyn Garden City (1919), while the eastern neighbourhood became uniformly tenemental, the communal gardens in the centre being reduced to a small public square.

Once the basic layout plan had been established, the Maxwells took great pains to ensure a first class residential

Left:-
Looking south-westwards over the tenements, villas and churches of Pollokshields (Derek Maxwell).

7

district. As an early and effective form of planning control, the Nether Pollok Estate laid down strict feu conditions to control the position, quality and use of all the buildings. In West Pollokshields, shops and trade were forbidden and no two villas were permitted to be exactly alike (although, in some cases, the actual differences amounted to no more than altering the entrance porch, adding a conservatory, surmounting the structure with a billiards room or just reversing the layout of the building!).

Nevertheless, the architectural styles which resulted range from Classical to Italianate, 'Glasgow Style' to Gothic and from Scots Baronial to 'Old English'. Many of the prominent architects of the late Victorian period are represented – Alexander 'Greek' Thomson, H. E. Clifford, W. F. McGibbon, H. & D. Barclay and Rowand Anderson among them. Many straightforward facades hide interiors richly adorned by the finest craftsmen, some of international renown. Stained, painted and figured glass abounds; as do ornamental plasterwork, cast iron and marble features, magnificent tiling, decorative mosaic flooring and a profusion of intricately carved and elegantly turned wood.

Right:-
Pollokshields in 1858, as shown on the first six-inch Ordnance Survey map (Trustees of the National Library of Scotland).

Below:-
Feuing plan for Pollokshields by David Rhind, 1849 (City Archives).

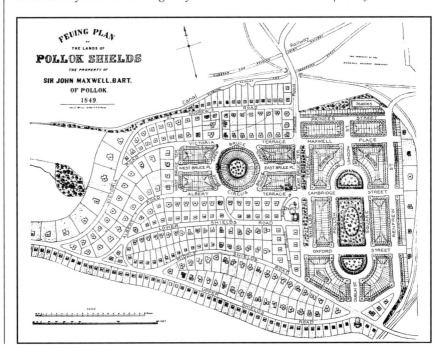

8

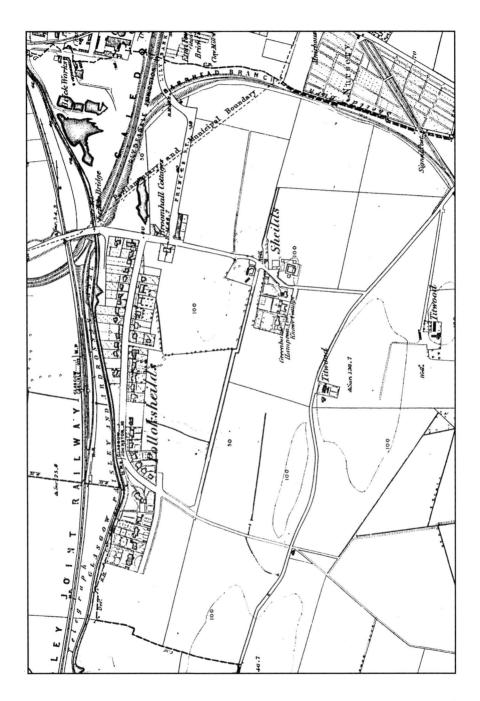

Villa Development in Pollokshields

The villa development began in 1851 and gradually spread southwards from the canal. When Maxwell Park was opened in 1890, West Pollokshields had over 400 villas. Between 1888 and 1907, the most prolific villa builders were James Marr (58 houses) and George Hamilton (68) – in their day, speculative developers of high quality housing. Clearly in competition with one another, they always employed Alexander Petrie and Fryers & Penman, respectively, as architects.

By 1910, West Pollokshields as we know it today was substantially completed with the construction of some of the biggest and most opulent houses in the avenues on the western fringes. As far back as 1893, the local press recorded that "all appear to be built in the most extravagant style. Where the people come from who occupy these palaces is a mystery...?" In fact, they were the denizens of trade and industry – iron founders and merchants, mantle makers, wholesalers, commission agents, ships' chandlers, hatters and confectioners as well as stockbrokers and even a pawnbroker. Prospering professionals, like lawyers and teachers, first resident in the tenement closes, often moved over to the villas.

Over the years, the area has acquired a mantle of mature trees, mainly limes and sycamores – a priceless asset which sometimes gives the false impression that the area was wooded immediately prior to its development (although it had been in prehistoric times). Before the advent of smokeless zones, Pollokshields in the centre of the wooded belt between Bellahouston Park and Queen's Park was often called the

Bird's eye view westwards over Maxwell Park and the surrounding villas of West Pollokshields (Pollokshields Heritage).

'Lung of Glasgow'! Some roads in West Pollokshields are further enhanced by kerbside trees; the City Council is now pursuing a modest programme of replacement and extension of provision.

Tenemental Pollokshields

The more level eastern area was mainly developed over the period 1855-1910 in a grid street pattern, still with wide roads and pavements, as an upmarket area of tenement flats, limited by feu contract to three-storeys in height rather than the four-storey more usual in Scottish cities. The flats are relatively large, varying in size from three to seven rooms, with considerable variety of exterior detail and elaborate plaster ceilings and quality joinery within.

The first tenements in Pollokshields were built on the south side of Prince's (now McCulloch) Street, running eastwards from Shields Road. The original flats provided in such early tenements were very spacious, some being two-storey flats or maisonettes on the upper floors. The large proportions of all of these most accommodating and magnificent family flats (up to nine rooms) made them vulnerable to subdivision in later years. The later tenements, mainly south and west of Nithsdale Road, are some of the finest examples in existence anywhere in Scotland, having retained their good detailing and generous proportions, often containing mixes of four to six rooms. Contributing to the size mix are 'main-door' flats (having individual access to the street as well as a back door into the common entrance or 'close'), which have one room less than the flats above.

The Nether Pollok feu conditions prohibited shared or outside toilets and all flats were provided with baths from the outset, in complete contrast to the standard of provision in most contemporary tenemental housing elsewhere in the city. Tenement flats were invariably leased to tenants as a source of income for their owners, but, after the Second World War, when escalating property management costs cancelled out any profitability, owner-occupation gradually became the norm, all the owners in a close sharing responsibility for common repairs.

As well as the tenements, the neighbourhood east of Shields Road contains all of the facilities which had generally not been permitted in West Pollokshields – the shops, churches and schools. Provision for shops on the ground floor was also strictly regulated by the feu superiors – restricted to focal points such as Albert Drive, Maxwell Road/Shields Road and Nithsdale Road/Kildrostan Street.

Burgh Status and the Cathcart Circle

By 1870, the City of Glasgow was considering boundary extensions to take in the developing suburban areas. Local applications were made for burgh status, not only for reasons of local civic pride, but mainly for householders to avoid paying the relatively high city rates. The Burgh of Pollokshields, with a population of 1,518 and only including the western area of villas, was formed in 1876. The original application for burgh status had related to the whole of Pollokshields, but towards the end of the application process, the people of the tenemental eastern area declined to join. They considered that a separate arrangement would provide public administration at a lower cost to its inhabitants, not having to subsidise road mending, street cleansing and other services over the more dispersed villa area.

Four years later, East Pollokshields assumed separate burgh status with a population of 4,360. But these and other

Albert Drive, the tenemental 'main street' of Pollokshields, showing Pollokshields Primary School on the right and the tower of St. Albert's Church in the background.

burghs were seen as a hindrance to city expansion, and, in 1891, parliamentary legislation enabled the extension of Glasgow's boundaries to include the whole of Pollokshields, as well as the other nearby southside burghs of Crosshill and Govanhill. By this time, the population of West Pollokshields had increased to 3,798, and East Pollokshields had 6,681 residents.

Before the start of the community's development, a small, roughly triangular piece of ground in the north-east corner, shown on the 1858 Ordnance Survey map, was already within Glasgow's municipal boundary. This corner was never developed for housing and, instead, became established as an industrial area providing Pollokshields with service trades such as builders, joiners and wheelwrights.

The extension of the Cathcart Railway to form the Cathcart Circle, started in 1890 and opened in 1894, added impetus to the development of Pollokshields – in anticipation of this, the Nether Pollok Estate had released land for the railway at agricultural rather than development value. The railway was constructed in a cutting between the new Maxwell Park and Pollokshields West Stations, minimising disturbance to future residents of nearby property, and the cutting was lined on either side by roads opening up the southern edges of Pollokshields for development.

Towards the end of the 19th century, the character of Pollokshields we know today was well established – villas, tenements and public buildings had been built of sandstone – generally blond or yellow locally-sourced material from the Giffnock quarries for the earlier developments and red sandstone from Ballochmyle (Ayrshire) and Locharbriggs (Dumfriesshire) for the later. Trees in streets, gardens and open spaces were beginning to make an impact, and church spires added interest to the skyline. The area's leafy winding streets of villas and its superior tenements were a reflection of the city's late Victorian and Edwardian prosperity.

Pollokshields in the 20th Century

Both tenement and villa developments were increasingly upmarket in the early part of the century. There was no reduction in either dwelling or plot sizes, rather the reverse. And generally, Edwardian tenements and villas incorporated even more diversity of style and richness of detail than in those of the Victorian era.

In the inter-war period, there was a lull in development with several substantial sites between villas dating from the turn of the century remaining vacant. By the 1950s, post-war shortages of materials, changed fortunes and a sparser population resulted inevitably in considerable neglect. Smoke from railways and domestic chimneys had also blackened and damaged many of the buildings. But, in 1962, Pollokshields became a smokeless zone under the Clean Air Act and, over the subsequent thirty years, the availability of housing improvement grants led to an enormous amount of stone cleaning, back court improvements and rehabilitation of property, greatly enhancing the area's appearance and revitalising interest in it.

In West Pollokshields, a post-war slackening in demand for large family housing, the non-availability of domestic staff, and high maintenance costs led to the subdivision of villas or their conversion into institutions such childrens' homes, religious orders, and nursing homes. At the same time, the remaining vacant sites on the western fringes of the area were gradually built up, partly with blocks of privately owned flats and latterly with speculative developments of standard English house types. East Pollokshields has also been subject to a number of less than ideal infill developments, using facing brick and concrete tile, while the area has never really recovered from the unnecessary removal of all of its 'non-essential' railings early in the Second World War.

Four of Pollokshields' original ten church buildings have gone completely. Two were transferred out of the area stone by stone for re-erection elsewhere and two have been destroyed by fire. Another has been converted into a nursing home, while a new mosque was built in 1990, reflecting altered patterns of worship over the last thirty years. The Pollokshields West railway station building was demolished in the late 1980s, but all other public buildings remain in place.

Redevelopment and Conservation

The greatest impact on the area in this century began in the 1950's when the then Glasgow Corporation acquired villas throughout Pollokshields to provide land for higher density council housing development. Most of the villas compulsorily purchased were the oldest examples, along St. Andrew's Drive and the north side of Maxwell Drive. By 1969, some 560 local authority flats in five- and eight-storey blocks had replaced the original villas at St. Andrew's Drive, which had included four by Alexander 'Greek' Thomson. As a result, only eleven of the original villas shown on the 1858 Ordnance Survey map still remain. Today, it is hard to believe that a high quality residential area would be considered for replacement by flat-roofed, deck-access flats, not only for aesthetic reasons, but because the *shortage* of high-quality, upmarket housing within the City boundary is now recognised as an issue.

Elsewhere in the area, many of the villas acquired by the Corporation were either converted for institutional use or, in Sheila Ogilvie's words, "left to become derelict and overgrown, creating eyesores in the district and threatening the value of well-tended neighbouring properties". By 1965,

local concern was channelled into the formation of the Pollokshields Preservation & Development Association. Supported by a 500-strong membership, it persuaded the Corporation to halt their acquisition of further properties and to sell several derelict villas back to the Association. Most of them were then sold on to private individuals, but numbers 54 and 56 Dalziel Drive, which were in a particularly bad state of neglect, were demolished to create space for two blocks of modern flats (Dalziel Court).

Although these particular new buildings were in themselves out of keeping with their surroundings, there

Aerial photograph showing the contrast between the redevelopment area at St. Andrew's Drive and the kind of villas that the new flats replaced (Derek Maxwell).

16

followed a significant turning point in the fortunes of Pollokshields. The Corporation was now convinced of the need to preserve the area's character, and both the tenemental and villa parts (East and West Pollokshields respectively) were designated Conservation Areas in 1973, protecting the trees as well as the buildings. West Pollokshields Conservation Area has furthermore been declared 'Outstanding' for the purposes of grant aid from Historic Scotland, the Government's historic buildings agency. Piecemeal infill development within the villa areas is now strictly controlled through statutory Local Plan policies which seek to preserve building lines, regulate the use of appropriate building materials and ensure that house and plot sizes are in keeping with local tradition. The Local Plan also encourages a reduction in the institutional use of properties, to further restore the residential character of the area.

1992 saw the formation of Pollokshields Heritage, a very active conservation and amenity society prompted by local concern about the deterioration of the Burgh Hall and Maxwell Park Railway Station and by persistent threats of undesirable development. Thanks to Lottery and other sources of finance, the Burgh Hall and its Lodge House have been renovated at a cost of over £1 million. Answering the need for local communication, Pollokshields Heritage publishes a quarterly newsletter distributed to over 6,000 homes throughout Pollokshields, together with the adjacent conservation area neighbourhoods of Dumbreck and Strathbungo.

The villa area in particular is benefiting from increased investment in property maintenance and reconversion of subdivided villas into single family houses, while future development of the Tramway Arts Centre in Albert Drive may act as a catalyst for more rapid regeneration in East Pollokshields. In a general sense, the area has, over the last thirty years or so, acquired a more cosmopolitan air, now housing one of the two main communities of people of Asian descent in Scotland. Asian influence is apparent in many parts of Pollokshields where shops, places of worship and investment in housing reflect its new multicultural character.

Pollokshields has remained remarkably intact, the Maxwells' original plans for the suburb being ever relevant. Its value as a high quality residential area so close to Glasgow's City Centre will become more significant as modes of transport change in the next century.

THE WALK

Suggested start and finish: Maxwell Park Railway Station.
Approximate duration of walk:

> Main Route: At least 2 hours
> Extension to Main Route: About 1 hour, 30 minutes.

1. Maxwell Park Station

Opened in 1894 when the Cathcart Railway was extended to become the Cathcart Circle, this station, with its Victorian 'vernacular' building, is handsomely located in a shallow cutting, now overlooked from the south by superior red sandstone tenements and bordered to the north by the park from which it takes its name. When first opened, the station saw wagons delivering masonry blocks for new villas and tenements, while, for many years, a bookstall on the ground floor was the neighbourhood's sole shop. Prize-winning flower beds and hanging baskets were a feature of the station until the mid 1960s and electrification (first suggested in 1899!) was introduced in 1961. But the bookstall had closed by the late 1970s and the station was 'destaffed' in 1986, although the stationmaster's house (some 500 yards along the line to the south) was inhabited for a few more years. The building was listed (category 'B') in 1990, and efforts subsequently began to find a new occupier, with the Railway Heritage Trust interested in promoting its restoration. The day may yet come when a fire once again burns brightly in the waiting room!

Mount the stairs to street level – where the spacious office accommodation housed the ticket office, and even porters in the early days! Turn right towards Terregles Avenue, and cross the

*Maxwell Park Station
(John Paton).*

road to the entrance of Maxwell Park. Once in the park, the pond can be seen on the far left.

2. Maxwell Park (See photograph on page 11)

This 21 acre park was gifted to the Burgh of Pollokshields by Sir John Stirling Maxwell of Nether Pollok in 1888. Sir John formally opened the park, along with the Burgh Hall at the south-east corner, in 1890. The park was formed from a marshy area of ground and the pond was created through drainage of both spring and surface water to its lowest part. In summer, it was a popular venue for sailing model yachts and, in the winter, for skating. 2,000 skaters were counted one day in 1895 on the frozen pond! Some of the planting was rearranged by the city authorities after 1891 to allow visitors a better view of the surrounding villas "with their ornamental pleasure grounds"! Its most prominent feature used to be the Hamilton Fountain (1908-1989), made of 'Carrara' stoneware by Doulton's Pottery. Also gone are the original bandstand, a drinking well, boats on the pond, a tennis pavilion and a putting green – all lost over the past few decades as the result of a combination of under-use, neglect, vandalism and lack of civic funds. But the formal gardens are well-maintained and the children's play area has been upgraded through local community initiative. Since 1992, the park has become the venue for an annual 'summer fayre' under the auspices of Pollokshields Heritage.

Take the long central pathway which runs through the heart of the park, bearing to the right until the Burgh Hall is reached.

3. Pollokshields Burgh Hall

At the eastern end of Maxwell Park stands Pollokshields Burgh Hall which, along with the associated Lodge and park gates, is listed as of national architectural/historic interest (category 'A'). Designed in the elaborate Scots 'renaissance' style of the 17th century by H. E. Clifford, this impressive public building is a physical reminder of the local pride once associated with burgh status. It was completed in 1890, just before the demise of the Burghs of Pollokshields and East Pollokshields. It is built of red sandstone from Ballochmyle, Ayrshire and features a tower with a cap-house and turret, oriel and Venetian windows and an interesting interior. The windows are extensively adorned with leaded and stained glass, all gifted by local residents. The first occupants of the two flats in the Lodge were the Pollokshields Burgh Sanitary Inspector and the Park Keeper.

After a long period of local authority ownership, including a period during the 1970s when it was used as an occupational day centre by the Social Work Department, the Hall was acquired in 1991 by a local charitable trust which embarked on fund raising towards the substantial restoration work required. The building was one of the very first recipients of Heritage Lottery funding (£400,000) for essential fabric repairs and the restoration of the Lodge as two flats; this work was completed over the winter of 1996-7 at a total cost of over £1 million.

Pass through the ornamental park gates at the side of the Hall to view the whole building. Take either exit, turn left and bear right at the fork, keeping to the south pavement all along the rising ground of Glencairn Drive.

4. 'The Twelve Apostles'
Unique in the area is the semi-circular block of villas on the right, bounded by Terregles Avenue, Glencairn Drive and Glencairn Gardens. Their local name, the 'Twelve Apostles', has no attributable derivation, but it may just have been a marketing whim! Dating from 1894-98, they were designed for James Marr by his usual architect, Alexander Petrie. Each bay-windowed symmetrical facade features an arcaded or columned porch, although some have a small tower at the side and several are built with the uncommon use of both red and blond sandstone.

5. Glencairn Drive
The north (or left) side of Glencairn Drive was developed around 1885. Shortly afterwards, Sir John Stirling Maxwell responded positively to a request by local residents that the south side of the street should be set aside for recreation. Accordingly, the Titwood Bowling and Tennis Club was established in May 1890 with two bowling greens, six tennis courts and a handsome, half-timbered pavilion. Opposite the bowling greens, the semi-detached villa at 50-52 Glencairn Drive is a particularly attractive and striking example, with its round headed windows, deep eaves and a low porch on each flank. Beyond Leslie Road, on the right hand corner, is the former site of Titwood Church of Scotland, now occupied by an attractive children's playground. The building was dismantled stone by stone and re-erected in Meiklerig Crescent in the Pollok housing scheme in 1954.

Pass the entrance to the modern flats and turn right into Shields Road for a few yards to view...

6. Fragment of Glencairn Church

Pollokshields Square is a flatted development on the site of the former Glencairn Church (vacated in 1977, burnt down in 1988 and originally built as the Trinity United Presbyterian Church, hence the builder's marketing name for the development – Trinity Square). Just round the corner into Shields Road, the main entrance arch of the former church can be seen at the top of the bank, relocated and preserved as a feature of the new development. Dating from 1891, the church and its rich furnishings were designed by W. G. Rowan. Many items, and some of the high-quality stained glass, were saved by the City Museums and Art Galleries Department.

Turn around and head northwards up Shields Road, noting the role of this street as the boundary between the villas to the west, and the tenements to the east.

7. Tenements at 689-709 Shields Road

Beyond Glencairn Drive, the buildings on the right are an appropriate introduction to the three-storey Pollokshields tenements. This particular block, dating from 1883 and originally known as Olrig Terrace, has frontages to three streets with bowed and turretted bays, classical details over the doors and windows, and corner turrets with truncated conical roofs. Just beyond are triangular green spaces left over when the 19th century street layout met awkwardly with

Looking north up Shields Road.

22

the much older route of Nithsdale Road, passing diagonally through Strathbungo, Pollokshields and Dumbreck.
Turn second left into Nithsdale Road.

8. Villa – 161 Nithsdale Road

Almost immediately on the left, on an elevated site, is a two storey and basement villa in the Greek style of Alexander Thomson (also known as 'Thomsonesque') with a symmetrical twin pedimented front and a porch with Ionic columns. This house was used as a synagogue for over half a century previous to its present role as a Mosque and Islamic School. The former villa next door has been converted into a Sikh Temple, again reflecting Pollokshields' multi-cultural character.

9. Former Church – 620 Shields Road

On the opposite side of the junction between Nithsdale Road and Shields Road is an impressive former church, designed to seat 1020 people, but now converted into a geriatric nursing home. Built in 1875-76 as a Free Church to the design

The Greek-style former church at 620 Shields Road.

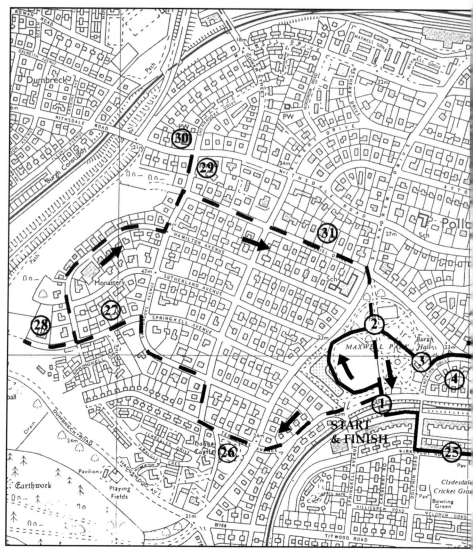

POLLOKSHIELDS – Map showing the layout of the area and the route of the Heritage Walk.

Scale:- 1:10,000 approx (6 inches to 1 mile).

No.	Place of Interest	Listed Category			
1.	Maxwell Park Station	B	12.	Pollokshields Church of Scotland & Hall	B
2.	Maxwell Park		13.	Pollokshields Primary School	B
3.	Pollokshields Burgh Halls	A	14.	Albert Cross	B*
4.	'Twelve Apostles'		15.	St Albert's RC Church and Hall	B
5.	Glencairn Drive		16.	Forth Street	
6.	Fragment of Glencairn Church	C(S)	17.	Industrial Building – 100 Albert Drive	B
7.	Tenements at 689-709 Shields Road	B	18.	Pollokshields District Library	B
8.	Villa – 161 Nithsdale Road	B	19.	Maxwell Square	
9.	Former Church – 620 Shields Road	B	20.	Pollokshields Primary School Annexe	B
10.	Terraced Housing – 553-609 Shields Road	B	21.	Tenements at Kenmure Street/	
11.	The Knowe	A		NithsdaleRoad/Darnley Street	B

24

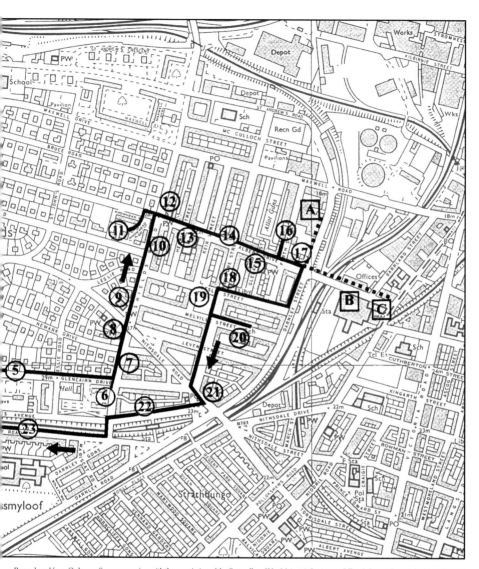

22.	Tenements at 44-84 Terregles Avenue	C(S)
23.	Tenements at 17-57 Fotheringay Road	B
24.	Pollokshields Congregational Church	C(S)
25.	Tenements at Kirkcaldy Road	

▬▬▬ EXTENSION TO MAIN ROUTE.

26.	Haggs Castle	B
27.	110 Springkell Avenue – 'Kelmscott'	B
28.	124 Springkell Avenue – 'Beneffrey'	A
29.	11 Sherbrooke Avenue – Sherbrooke Castle Hotel	B
30.	Sherbrooke St Gilbert's Church	B
31.	Villas – 38-42 Dalziel Drive	B

■■■■ OFFSHOOTS FROM MAIN ROUTE

Letter	Place of Interest	Listed Category
A.	Office Building – 46-50 Darnley Street	A
B.	The Tramway (Theatre)	B
C.	St Ninian's Episcopal Church	B

* Except north-west corner.

25

of McKissack & Rowan, the building later became Pollokshields West Church (of Scotland) and subsequently – for 25 years – the Nithsdale Trust Church of the Plymouth Brethren. Again in a 'Thomsonesque' Greek style, it is notable for its hexastyle (six-columned) upper Ionic porticos with pediments and its tall, lantern-topped corner tower, 170 feet high. The adjacent semi-detached villa in Shields Road has interesting columned and fret-worked porches, cast-iron window balconies and a shallow-pitched roof.

Proceed further along Shields Road.

10. Terraced Housing – 553-609 Shields Road

On the right, after the junction with Leslie Street, is one of only two rows of Victorian terraced housing in Pollokshields. Further along Shields Road, at the crest of the hill, the other terrace eases the transition between the villas and tenements, but this first block is tenemental in scale. Originally called Knowe Terrace and dating from around 1875, its design was heavily influenced by 'Greek' Thomson's 'The Knowe' (next item) across the road. Worthy of note are the chimneypots based on The Knowe's gatepiers. The identity of the architect is unknown.

Before proceeding to the front of The Knowe, turn into Aytoun Road for a short distance to view, on the right, its back wall featuring fireclay balusters and Greek-style garden doorway, c.1873. Then return to Shields Road and continue along the block, turn left into Albert Drive and left again into Knowehead Gardens.

The terraced housing at 553-609 Shields Road.

The Knowe
(Eric Masterton).

11. The Knowe

At the end of the drive is situated The Knowe, the earliest surviving Glasgow villa designed by Alexander 'Greek' Thomson, begun in 1852. It was built in stages, conforming to a picturesque Italian style dropped by the architect around 1856. The architectural characteristics more commonly associated with Thomson's work – the broad eaves, the low pitched roofs – are much in evidence, complementing the open arched porch and the small tower or campanile.

It was built for John Blair of J. & W. A. Blair, cap and hat manufacturers of 125 Trongate, and was situated immediately to the west of the original line of Shields Road and adjacent to the old farm of Shields. It was the first villa to be erected away from St. Andrew's Drive where the earliest villas in the district were built in 1851. When Shields Farm was demolished around 1870, Shields Road was driven through on a more direct line and the opportunity was taken to enlarge the garden of The Knowe.

In the 1970s, after refusal of listed building consent for demolition, the building was returned to residential use, having been a Salvation Army Home for single mothers since 1941. At the same time, it lost its extensive grounds to the rather insensitively designed modern flats which now occupy

the site, the one concession in their design being the detailing of the concrete window lintels to reflect The Knowe's Romanesque arches. However, it retains its Albert Drive address and its charming two-storey lodge, similar in many respects to the house itself.

Leaving Knowehead Gardens, turn right and continue down Albert Drive, the 'main street' of Pollokshields.

12. Pollokshields Church of Scotland and Hall

This Gothic church at the corner with its clerestory, corner tower and spire was designed by Robert Baldie and dates from 1878. It was built at a cost of £14,000, a sum which represents only a tiny fraction of the cost of refurbishing the church in the 1980's. It replaced the adjoining and slightly older church hall at 525 Shields Road as the place of worship. The equally grand interior reflects Pollokshields' wealth in the quality of its furnishings and stained glass. The organ case, communion table, pulpit and pews are all magnificent

Above:-
'Kew Terrace'
cartouche, Herriet
Street.

Below:-
Pollokshields
Primary School,
Albert Drive.

and all in Perpendicular style. Also within the church are three framed, embroidered panels commemorating the late Chris K. Fletcher, the local architect whose architectural sketches adorn this guide. The present congregation is the result of amalgamations with Titwood Church (see Item 5), Glencairn Church (Item 6), Pollokshields West Church (Item 9), Albert Drive Church (Item 15) and Pollokshields Kenmure Church (still used as halls when it, too, succumbed to fire damage in 1983). On the Shields Road side of the church is an interesting war memorial of 1921, based on the Ruthwell and Bewcastle crosses.

A little way down Albert Drive, the pillar box at the corner with Herriet Street is a rare example carrying the insignia of King Edward VIII. Up above, on the Herriet Street frontage, can be seen the beautifully carved cartouche carrying the name 'Kew Terrace', a reminder of the original terrace names which have long since ceased to be official postal addresses.

13. Pollokshields Primary School
The second street block on the right is occupied by a building that has housed Albert Road Academy from 1902, Pollokshields Senior Secondary School from 1926 and the main part of Pollokshields Primary School since 1962 (see also Item 20). Originally dating from 1882 and designed by

H. & D. Barclay, it is a two-storey building in the Scottish Renaissance style, featuring triple windows with pilasters. These columns are fluted on the ground floor and have sculptured panels on the first.

14. Albert Cross
The second crossroads after Pollokshields Primary School, where Kenmure Street crosses Albert Drive at the traffic lights, is known as Albert Cross, always designed as the commercial focal point of Pollokshields and which soon became the centre of the Victorian Burgh of East Pollokshields. The tenement corner detail, with the conical or bell-shaped turrets above, reflects its importance.

Below (left):- Albert Cross Buildings.

Below (right):- St. Albert's RC Church, Albert Drive.

15. St. Albert's RC Church and Hall
On the right hand side, on the corner with Glenapp Street, stands St. Albert's RC Church, originally built as a presbyterian church in 1886, the architect being J. B. Wilson. Built in Italian Renaissance style, the dramatic tower is 140 feet high, featuring arcaded bell-stages and a dome. Between 1887 and 1909, it was known as the Stockwell Free Church, reflecting its relocation from the City Centre, and then as Albert Drive United Free Church until the congregation joined the Church of Scotland in 1929. In 1965, the building was sold to the Roman Catholic Church and the two-storey

presbytery diagonally opposite was built. At the end of the short stretch of Glenapp Street on the left, a little green door in the wall gives access to the New Victoria Gardens – allotments which were 'New' when they were established here over a hundred years ago in 1871, having started in Govanhill in 1865 (as the Victoria Gardens). There are 60 plots, cultivated by enthusiasts of all ages. An annual Flower Show and Open Day, a tradition begun in 1887, still continues.

16. Forth Street
On the next left, Forth Street contains a considerable variety of building forms and activities. On the left-hand side, a modern pair of semi-detached houses precedes a small group of cottages, somewhat altered, but of a type relatively rare in the City of Glasgow. They were originally occupied by horse-cab hirers, and, although they look older, map evidence indicates that these cottages are roughly contemporary with the surrounding development of Pollokshields. Opposite is a new mosque, built in facing brick and featuring distinctive round-headed windows.

17. Industrial Building – 100 Albert Drive
Back in Albert Drive, on the left hand corner with Darnley Street, are the premises of Hugh Fulton Electrical Ltd. This was custom built in 1895 as the Glasgow Steam Laundry and Carpetbeating Works which for 60 years performed mechanically those chores usually undertaken by domestic staff. Since then it has housed dairy offices and an upholsterer's warehouse.

100 Albert Drive, originally the Glasgow Steam Laundry and Carpetbeating Works.

At this point, the main route of the heritage walk proceeds to the right, along Darnley Street. Items of interest can, however, be found through short diversions to the left (Item A) and straight ahead (Items B and C).

Offshoots from Main Route

A. Office Building – 46-50 Darnley Street

This three-storey, ashlar-fronted commercial building, formerly the premises of Millar and Lang, was designed in 1902 by D. B. Dobson of Gordon & Dobson. The front is embellished with detail in the style of Charles Rennie Mackintosh. Consistent with its date, location and function, the sides are brick, unlike the general pattern in the residential parts of Pollokshields, where stone all round is the norm. But it is listed as of national architectural/historic interest (category 'A') because of its fine and exceptionally complete Art Nouveau office interiors on the first floor.

Art Nouveau office building at 46-50 Darnley Street. The lettering on the facade has been altered since the sketch was drawn.

B. The Tramway (Theatre)

Further along Albert Drive, beyond the entrance to Pollokshields East Station (from which walkers can travel back to the City Centre or around the Cathcart Circle) is the Tramway, a City Council venue notable, since 1989, for innovative and internationally-acclaimed theatrical productions, exhibitions of the latest in modern art and community events. Built as a tram depot, originally with stables (from the days of horse trams) on the first floor, it was the first home of the city's Transport Museum, prior to its present location at the Kelvin Hall. The building was designed by W. Clark of the Corporation Tramways Department and dates from 1894. Its use as a tram depot ceased after the last trams ran in 1962, but tram rails are still in situ as a reminder of its origin. Substantial improvements to performance and exhibition spaces are proposed.

The interior of St Ninian's Episcopal Church.

C. St Ninian's Episcopal Church
Still further along, on the right-hand corner with Pollokshaws Road, is St Ninian's Episcopal Church, designed by David Thomson in the early French Gothic style, and built over the period 1873-77. The main feature is the polygonal apse facing Pollokshaws Road with its gargoyles based on saints and prophets. The impressive interior is High Victorian with good furniture, mural painting and stained glass.

From Darnley Street, above the distant tenements on the left, can be seen the crown steeple of the former Strathbungo Parish Church. Turn first right into Leslie Street and continue up to Maxwell Square, with Pollokshields Library on the right, beyond the rather incongruous electricity sub-station.

18. Pollokshields Public Library
This library of 1907 was the competition-winning design of Thomas Gilmour of the City Engineer's Department. His designs were revised by his superior, A. B. McDonald; whether the changes were welcomed by Gilmour is not recorded! The Edwardian Baroque design of the exterior is enlivened by well carved cartouches and panels inscribed 'Literature; History; The Arts', while the interior has stained glass designed and made by John C. Hall. Costing about £5,000, it was one of twelve Glasgow libraries funded by Andrew Carnegie.

19. Maxwell Square
This square, much smaller than that originally envisaged as the centrepiece of east Pollokshields, covers three-quarters of an acre and was opened in 1889. The natural ground level was nine feet below that of the surrounding streets, but the surface had been raised by six feet and covered with ashes and fresh turf. With its cast iron drinking fountain and seats, it was considered a model children's playground of the time. However, by 1891, numerous complaints had been made

Pollokshields Public Library, Leslie Street.

The Annexe of Pollokshields Primary School, Melville Street.

about disorderly conduct taking place in the evenings. On the opposite (west) side of the square, the handsome red sandstone tenement of 1901 is notable for the round tower at each corner and the characteristic Glaswegian glazing pattern in the upper sashes of the windows – one relatively large pane in the centre, surrounded by eight smaller panes.

Turn left and proceed to the end of Kenmure Street, making a brief diversion to the left down Melville Street, to view the oldest purpose-built school in Pollokshields.

20. Pollokshields Primary School Annexe

Looking down Melville Street, a school building with its associated janitor's house can be seen halfway along on the right. First opened in 1879, this was Pollokshields Public School which became Pollokshields Primary School in 1926 and is now its infant department. Like the main school in Albert Drive, it was designed by H. & D. Barclay for Govan Parish School Board, some Greek influence being apparent below the first floor windows. On the 21st of March, 1882, a playground shelter at the school collapsed on top of about thirty children. Two girls were found dead, and another girl and a boy died shortly afterwards from their injuries. In May of that year, David Barclay, the architect, and four tradesmen were apprehended on a charge of culpable homicide in connection with the fatalities. Although, after court deliberation, the prisoners were set free on the criminal charge, Govan Parish School Board was found to be negligent through lack of supervision.

From the end of Kenmure Street, turn left into Nithsdale Road, noting the tenement block on the left.

Tenements in Nithsdale Road with Alexander Thomson's work in the foreground.

21. Tenements at Kenmure St./Nithsdale Rd./Darnley St.

This block of tenements, once known as Lorne Terrace, was designed by Alexander 'Greek' Thomson, begun in 1873 and completed by his partner, Robert Turnbull in 1888. The severe Greek style is simple and distinctive. Look back also at the handsome, curved tenement at the opposite corner of Kenmure Street and Nithsdale Road. The ground floor of this building was redesigned as a shopping parade in 1883, and neighbouring ground floor flats in Nithsdale Road were converted into shops, to cater for local demand.

Turn first right into Terregles Avenue, between two of the area's characteristic triangular green spaces.

22. Tenements at 44-84 Terregles Avenue

Like other tenements in Pollokshields, those south-west of Nithsdale Road, are generously proportioned, with four to six room dwellings as the norm. The flats of 1895 by H. E. Clifford at 44-84 Terregles Avenue are a good example of this. Built of fine-grained cream sandstone, complemented by a full, unaltered set of cream-painted window frames, this three-storey tenement is one of Glasgow's best examples of

Right:-
H. E. Clifford's
tenements at 44-
84 Terregles
Avenue.

Below:-
Plan of typical
ground floor
tenement layout,
Terregles Avenue – a
simplified version of
H. E. Clifford's
original drawing
(City Archives).

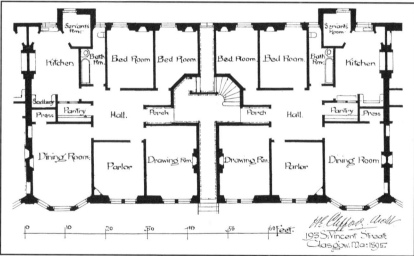

'modern movement' architecture. It features the paired bay windows, overhanging eaves and prominent downpipes and chimneystacks commonly associated with the 'Glasgow Style'. Of the original railings, only the stair balustrades on the Terregles Avenue frontage remain.

Halfway along this (the first) stretch of Terregles Avenue is Pollokshields West Station, a well-used halt on the Cathcart Circle. At the end of the block, turn left over the railway, and then immediately right into Fotheringay Road.

23. Tenements at 17-57 Fotheringay Road

Facing north across the cutting of the Cathcart Circle, this range of tenements, also by H. E. Clifford but constructed in red sandstone, is more elaborate, with varied bay window and balcony features, together with wavy parapets and a turret at the western end. The flats are large, containing 4-6 apartments, maid's room and bathroom. Window frames, in this instance, are still in their traditional, uniform green. At number 33 can be seen a bronze wall plaque, unveiled in 1993, marking the birthplace of James A. Mollison (1905-59), the pioneer aviator. He was the first person to make a successful non-stop, solo flight across the North Atlantic in the more difficult, westerly direction.

24. Pollokshields Congregational Church

Dating from 1903, this simple, towerless, red sandstone church in 'Gothic' mid-pointed style was designed by Steele & Balfour.

Turn left into Beaton Road. Before turning right into Kirkcaldy Road, note the modern buildings of Hutchesons' Grammar School on the left, their design not greatly different from contemporary state schools. This school was founded in 1795 at Ingram Street in the city centre and the Boys' School was situated in Crown Street, Hutchesontown from 1840 until 1959 when the redevelopment of the Gorbals and the need for more spacious accommodation forced its relocation to the current site. It became co-educational in 1976.

25. Tenements at Kirkcaldy Road

The Edwardian tenements in this street, dating from 1907-9 and containing 3-5 rooms, are said to contain the most magnificent 'wally' (ceramic tiled) closes in Pollokshields. There are several designs, mainly in varied greens, blues and pinks, which can be seen through the glazed security doors without leaving the pavement. It is interesting to note that, until recent years, few Glasgow tenements had a close door, unlike Edinburgh tenements where their provision was the norm. Sadly, Pollokshields exhibits little uniformity in the design of the now necessary security doors.

On the south side of the road are the Titwood Athletic Grounds, home of the Clydesdale Cricket Club since 1875, having been founded in Kinning Park in 1848. The pavilion, designed by H. E. Clifford, was built in 1904 when the grounds were extended. As the Clydesdale Cricket and Hockey Club, it has gained a good international reputation, and has recently formed an all-weather synthetic hockey

Edwardian tenements, Kirkcaldy Road.

pitch. At the end of the block, the scale of the buildings reduces abruptly, from tenements to bungalows, reflecting the change in middle-class housing preferences which became firmly established after World War I. Only now are serious attempts being made to reintroduce the traditional tenemental building form in the city.

Turn first right into Dolphin Road, then left into Fotheringay Road to return to Maxwell Park Station.

There are a number of other, more widely spaced, buildings of exceptional interest in the western part of Pollokshields. These can be visited by walking, cycling or motoring the extension to the main route described on the following pages.

Extension to Main Route

Leaving the northern entrance of Maxwell Park Station (as at the start of the main walk), turn left into Terregles Avenue. Cross Springkell Avenue, continue along the next section of Terregles Avenue, then fork right until St Andrew's Drive is reached.

26. Haggs Castle

On the opposite side of St. Andrew's Drive, in its own corner grounds and rather hidden by shrubbery, is Haggs Castle. By far the oldest building in Pollokshields, and dating from 1585, it is a remnant of a previous era when it stood in the open countryside beside the old Pollokshaws-Govan road, which remains as the lane to the west. The castle is a traditional Scottish three-storey rubble-built, L-plan towerhouse with richly carved detail at dormer heads and entrances. After the 1680s, it was used as a dower house for the ladies of the family, and in the mid 18th century, the family completed their move to Pollok House. The castle was abandoned and, by the 1840s, it was in ruinous condition with the ground floor in use as the smithy for a local colliery. In 1860, having been restored in a pronounced Victorian, Baronial style, it became the house and offices for the Estate Factor. After the factor's death in 1899, a drawing room,

Haggs Castle, 100 St Andrew's Drive.

billiard room and a new circular staircase were added and, from 1900 to 1943, the castle was let out as a single residence. It was requisitioned by the army in 1943, and, then, in the late 1940's, the Maxwell trustees converted it into flats. In 1972, it was bought by Glasgow Corporation and used as a children's museum for a number of years. Finally, in 1997, it was sold by the Council for use, once again, as a private dwellinghouse.

Continue west along Terregles Avenue, turn first right into Albert Drive, first left up Sherbrooke Avenue, and first left into Springkell Avenue. Along this rising ground are handsome villas, all unique in themselves.

'Kelmscott', 110 Springkell Avenue.

27. 110 Springkell Avenue – 'Kelmscott'

The third house on the right is 'Kelmscott', a splendid Arts and Crafts villa of 1902-03 which combines Glasgow Style elements with Scots Baronial and Queen Anne revival. The stained glass is the work of Oscar Paterson and the interior retains many of its original Art Nouveau fittings.

The house represents the first collaboration between the architect John Nisbet and his client, the celebrated builder John Auld Mactaggart. Nisbet was later employed by Mactaggart to design a series of tenements for his property companies in Hyndland, Broomhill, Shawlands, Alexandra Park (all Glasgow) and Gourock. Mactaggart trained in his uncle's sawmill in Pollokshields and later in the contracting firm of Robert Mickel & Co. of Bo'ness, Glasgow and London, leading to the founding of Mactaggart and Mickel, the well-known Scottish suburban house-builder.

The mixed character of the development further along the street well illustrates the prolonged time period between the start of developments on the western fringes of Pollokshields and their fairly recent completion.

28. 124 Springkell Avenue – 'Beneffrey'

On the right hand side, where Springkell Avenue ends, this large two-storey coursed rubble mansion of 1910, situated on the western extremity of Pollokshields, and one of the last such buildings to be constructed in the area, is notable for its large round tower and fine detailing. It was designed by William Hunter McNab, partner of, and successor to, William Leiper in his 'Franco-Scots Late Gothic' style, many examples of which can be found in Helensburgh. The house was built for John Anderson and is now subdivided into three private dwellings. The interior is more English in style – much oak panelling, low beamed ceilings and carved stone overmantels, together with high quality ornamental plasterwork.

Retrace your steps and turn left into Hamilton Avenue which, after the next junction, becomes uncharacteristically narrow for Pollokshields. Modern bungalows and villas on the left hand side contrast with older development on the right, occupying the most elevated site in the district and enjoying fine, open views to the north-west. Immediately after the Mount Carmel Monastery is a row of four villas, dating from 1896. These villas were the work of Fryers and Penman, architects, and George Hamilton, a local builder. Turn left again into Sherbrooke Avenue, down towards Nithsdale Road.

29. 11 Sherbrooke Avenue – Sherbrooke Castle Hotel

Before Nithsdale Road is reached, on the right can be seen the Sherbrooke Castle Hotel on its commanding, elevated site. This red sandstone mansion was constructed for himself by John Morrison, a contractor who prospered during the city's building boom. Dating from 1896 and designed by the architects Thomson & Sandilands, it is described in *Buildings of Scotland* as "the apotheosis of the Baronial style in Glasgow, utterly uninspired in detail and with an over-tall tower that makes a coarse and obvious impact". Readers/walkers may come to their own, more positive, conclusions! The building, along with neighbouring villas, was requisitioned by the Royal Navy during the Second World War and used as a radar training station – it was a ship that never put to sea.

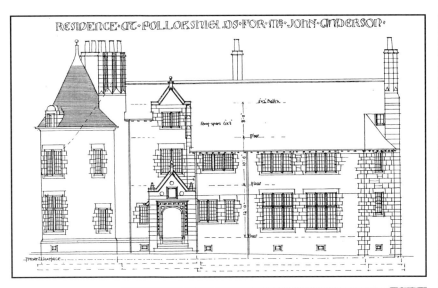

RESIDENCE·AT·POLLOKSHIELDS·FOR·Mr·JOHN·ANDERSON·

*Above:-
'Beneffrey', 124
Springkell Avenue:
William Hunter
McNab's original
drawing of the east
(entrance) elevation
(City Archives).*

*Right:-
Sherbrooke Castle
Hotel on its
elevated site at the
corner of Nithsdale
Road and
Sherbrooke
Avenue.*

30. Sherbrooke St Gilbert's Church

This church is prominently located to the left, on the opposite side of Nithsdale Road. Originally designed by W. F. McGibbon in early pointed 13th century Gothic style, it dates from 1894-99. The church's main features are its small double transept, its sculptured porch and its hammerbeam roof. Unfortunately, it was recently burnt out by fire following an accident during roof repairs. The church was well insured, however, and its subsequent restoration includes newly commissioned stained glass windows.

Retrace your steps for a short distance up Sherbrooke Avenue, then turn left into Dalziel Drive. On the right hand near corner with Albert Drive is Somersby (No. 31), an attractive Arts and Crafts villa with Baronial and Tudor elements. It was designed by H.E. Clifford and dates from 1902.

31. Villas – 38-42 Dalziel Drive

Between Albert Drive and St. Andrew's Drive, the villas in Dalziel Drive exhibit a contrast between the exuberant and unorthodox Scottish Baronial style of numbers 38, 40 and 42 on the north side and the relatively formal Edwardian villas on the other. 'Dykeneuk' (No. 40), said to have been built circa 1886, is perhaps the most unusual with its chamfered corners and a diagonal arch linking the chimneystack and crow-stepped gable.

From the crossroads with St. Andrew's Drive, walkers should enter Maxwell Park at the corner, and follow the path right through to the starting point at Maxwell Park Station. Owing to the road closure at the end of this section of Dalziel Drive, drivers should find an alternative route to the end of the 'trail'.

Other Notable Villas in Pollokshields

Although not situated on the route of the Heritage Walk, mention should be made of three further villas in Pollokshields designed by Alexander 'Greek' Thomson. In

202 Nithsdale Road, designed by Alexander Thomson (City Planning and Development Archives).

Nithsdale Road are two adjacent, category 'A' listed houses, unfortunately rather hidden from the street by trees and dense shrubbery. Number 202, dating from 1870, is remarkably austere and deliberately lacking in external ornamentation, with, in contrast, the diminutive Egyptian-style 'Ellisland' next door at number 200, built a year later. Below the latter's shallow pitched roof can be seen its impressive front entrance, the door being flanked by lotus-headed columns and bulbous cast-iron lamp standards placed on broad, stone plinths. There is also a posthumously completed 'Greek' Thomson double villa at 336-338 Albert Drive, while, as stated earlier in this guide, four early examples at St Andrew's Drive did not survive the 1960s.

The front entrance of 'Ellisland', 200 Nithsdale Road, another of 'Greek' Thomson's works (City Planning and Development Archives).

References

'Pollokshields Pastiche' by Sheila M. Ogilvie, 1989.

'Pollokshields Panorama' by Sheila M. Ogilvie, 1990.

'Pollokshields' – Interim Report by the Pollokshields Preservation and Development Association Ltd., Glasgow, May 1966.

'Going... Gone... To Come' by Donald MacDonald, *Weekly Scotsman,* 11th July 1963.

'How the Pollokshields Preservation and Development Association Began... and What has been Done in Six Years', *Pollokshields Gazette,* October 1970.

'The Buildings of Scotland – Glasgow' by Elizabeth Williamson, Anne Riches & Malcolm Higgs, Penguin Books, London, 1990.

'The Cathcart Line' by Jack Kernahan, Scottish Railway Preservation Trust, Falkirk, 1980.

'The Glasgow Tenement' by Frank Worsdall, Richard Drew Publishing, Glasgow, 1989.

'Glasgow – The Forming of the City', edited by Peter Reed, Edinburgh University Press, 1993.

'The Imperial Gazetteer of Scotland', edited by John Marius Wilson, A. Fullarton & Co, London and Edinburgh, c. 1867.

'Rambles Round Glasgow' by Hugh MacDonald, 1854.

Further Recommended Reading

'Queen's Park – Historical Guide and Heritage Walk', Glasgow City Council, 1996.

'Architecture of Glasgow' by Andor Gomme and David Walker, Lund Humphries, 1987.

'Charles Rennie Mackintosh – His Buildings In and Around Glasgow' (Heritage Trail) (Seventh Edition), City of Glasgow Council, 1996.

'Alexander "Greek" Thomson – The Glasgow Buildings' (Heritage Trails), City of Glasgow District Council, 1990.

'The Life and Work of Alexander Thomson' by Ronald McFadzean, Routledge & Kegan Paul, London, 1979.

'"Greek" Thomson' edited by Gavin Stamp and Sam McKinstry, Edinburgh University Press, 1994.

'The City that Disappeared – Glasgow's Demolished Architecture' by Frank Worsdall, Molendinar Press, 1981.

Architectural Glossary

An attempt has been made to avoid the use of architectural jargon in this guide, but where technical terms have been unavoidable, their definitions are set out below.

Apse:	Semi-circular (in plan) end of building, especially church.
Arts and Crafts:	Architectural style incorporating various English traditional vernacular characteristics.
Ashlar:	Masonry of large blocks with even faces and square edges.

Balustrades:	Handrails and their vertical supports.
Cap-house:	Small chamber at top of tower, reached by spiral staircase.
Cartouche:	Tablet with ornate frame, bearing coat of arms or inscription.
Clerestory:	Upper storey of the walls of a church, pierced by windows.
Double Villa:	Semi-detached villa of superior quality, composition often asymmetrical.
Glasgow Style:	Variations of Art Nouveau peculiar to certain Glasgow architects around the year 1900.
Pediment:	Formalised classical gable, also used over doors, windows, etc.
Perpendicular:	Style of English Gothic architecture (c. 1335-1530).
Pilaster:	Column of rectangular rather than circular cross-section.
Portico:	Porch with detached columns.
Rubble:	Masonry with stones wholly or partly in a rough state.

Acknowledgements

The author would like to thank the many people who contributed to the production of this guide and is particularly indebted to Sheila Ogilvie and Karin Currie for their local knowledge, for their assistance in ensuring accuracy and for suggesting improvements to the text.

The author is extremely grateful for May Fletcher's permission to reproduce the line drawings of her late husband, Chris K. Fletcher, an architect who had a particular fondness for the buildings of Pollokshields. Except where indicated after the captions, the photographs were taken by the author. Thanks are also due to Iain Paterson, Tim Mitchell, Jean Morrison, David Horner, Maureen Lanigan and Stephen Turnbull of Glasgow City Council, and to Dr. Thomas C. Welsh, for their assistance.

Every effort has been made to secure permission to include material in this book; in this connection, the assistance of Glasgow Libraries and Archives and the Trustees of the National Library of Scotland was very welcome. The publisher apologises for any errors or significant omissions and would be grateful to be notified of any corrections.

The guide was designed by Margaret McBride, graphic designer, Glasgow Libraries and Archives, whose collaboration with the author was greatly appreciated, and was printed by Cordfall Limited. Its production was funded by the Council's South Area Committee as a contribution towards Glasgow 1999, UK City of Architecture and Design.

The author is a Senior Planning Officer in the Urban Regeneration Division of Glasgow City Council's Planning and Development Department; it has to be noted that any views expressed are not necessarily those of the Council.